Into The Light

By Akal Sahai Singh
(Steve Coffing)

Author: Steve Coffing (Akal Sahai Singh)

Covers: Steve Coffing

Website: www.bethelighthouse.com

First published by Dog Ear Publishing
4010 W. 86th Street, Ste H
Indianapolis, IN 46268
www.dogearpublishing.net

ISBN: 978-145750-220-0

This book is printed on acid-free paper.

Printed in the United States of America

Disclaimer

The information contained in this book comes from my impressions and interpretations of what I've experienced while practicing Kundalini Yoga and White Tantric Yoga.

Nothing in this book should be construed as medical advice. While Bound Lotus and the meditations and yoga sets mentioned in this book have benefited many, this book makes no claim to diagnose, treat, cure or prevent any disease, illness, or other condition.

Always check with your personal physician or licensed health care practitioner before making any significant modifications to your lifestyle, to insure that the lifestyle changes, are appropriate for your personal health condition and consistent with any medication you may be taking.

It is recommended that you receive instruction from a KRI certified Kundalini Yoga teacher before attempting any of the postures, kriyas, or meditations mentioned in this book.

For the Light

Foreword

I am lucky enough to have known Akal Sahai Singh for many years now, and enjoyed his company at many Solstice celebrations. I find it very inspiring to know people who have the desire and discipline to make the teachings of Yogi Bhajan a part of their daily life, and who, like Akal Sahai, exhibit a radiance and generosity of spirit that our Teacher would be proud of. Not many can capture the delight they find in the experience of their practice; Akal Sahai does just that in Into the Light.

Nam Kaur Khalsa

YOGIC REALITY INC.

Introduction

I'd intentionally delayed the ending of this book for quite some time, wanting, waiting for something momentous to happen, focusing on what I did not have, rather than the Infinite blessings that I do have.

It's not about the destination or what you think you need, it's about stepping into the Light, it's about making a difference in the life of another, it's about being the Lighthouse.

Do that one thing and you will be blessed beyond your wildest dreams!

~Sat Nam,

Akal Sahai Singh

January 3, 2011

Someone special

City on the water, angels, eagles, mountaintop homes, light….

Laughter echoes across the Infinite. Time, space, energy – Infinite are we.

Laugh and live.

Live in the glow

Would that I could explain….

Strained my back at the gym – somehow – pain knifed down my leg… I couldn't move… at one point, I sneezed and thought I was paralyzed….

I realized that it didn't matter whether the journey resulted in enlightenment or not, just that I made it home.

The next morning I folded myself up and chanted the pain away, today I feel even better….

May you always live in the glow, may the light carry you through any pain and may you be, Infinite.

Sat Nam Ji.

Akal Sahai Singh

7/16/08

Commitment to change

*P*rosperity, Day 1…

Write itself it must, flow….

My intention, to prosper, my commitment – to prosperity.

The commitment, as ever, to change, to be the lighthouse, to be, the Light.

Sat Nam.

Live long and prosper

*P*rosperity, Day 5….

Simple commitment to 1,000 days of a prosperity meditation, not to dabble – a commitment.

Not to want….

How something so basic can create such a shift in one's existence!

May we all live long and prosper.

Sat Nam Ji!

Brothers and sisters

Worlds of difference between knowing it, feeling it and living it… began to call them, "Brother," not just think of my fellow man as such….

I chose healing and it was so, I chose prosperity and it was.

May you always choose well.

Sat Nam.

For Sat Purusha

"Good! I'm so glad to hear that, you deserve good things because you are wonderful AND everyone who comes across you loves you."

I smiled as I basked in the glow of a dear friends words... vowing to stay in the space they put me into, till Infinity, until I am the light.

Sat Nam Sat Purusha, Sat Nam and thank you!

To freedom

Japji pervades the soul, rebuilding your existence at a cellular level... recreating your being, of the light....

Here's to ever higher awakenings, to realizations grand and otherwise, here's to freedom, may we all find it.

Sat Nam.

Ardas

Words of a friend echo throughout my being...

"Universe, please bring me what you think best for me," Nam said as she spoke of being careful what we ask for.

Two things you can plan on, the sun rising and my being at Solstice, beyond that, "Universe, please bring me what you think best for me."

Sat Nam.

Look for me

Wherever you see the light, I'll be there.

Even in the dark, I'll be there.

I am the light, and so are you.

Sat Nam.

Into the light

I stepped into the light, and saw the perfection in all things….

I quit asking the universe for what I had once so wanted and instead asked it to bring me whatever it thought best for me.

I wonder, what it'll bring… let's find out, let's all step into the light and see what it brings us.

The boatman

I am the boatman, I am change, I am the light, I am, I am.

Looking forward

I couldn't begin to count how many times I heard, "Good to see you," this Solstice past.

What especially stands out though, is Tully saying, "I was hoping you'd be here," as he enfolded me in the biggest of hugs....

May we all meet again, by the lake of Truth....

Sat Nam.

At journey's end

I brought back a stone from the top of the world.

It looks volcanic, and yet, I found it in the desert....

How often, we know not, what awaits us, at our journey's end....

Home, is where my backpack is, everything else, it just is.

Sat Nam Ji.

What lay beyond?

I wonder, of my angels....

I mean, what part of me lives in their world and what part of them lives in mine?

Now I know, within that, I've answered my own question, but still… what lay beyond what is seen?

Of wishes and dreams

*I*f you could have any one thing, what would it be? What would you wish for?

Would it be, that she say, "Yes," and give you her heart, or would you wish for the light? Would you wish at all?

What if every day were more beautiful than the last, what dreams we'd realize! Wahe Guru!

Hari Ram

*A*n angel phoned in the night, to chant, to prosper, and to be Infinite. To share in my evening….

I've prospered beyond measure, for I have the best of friends. Equally blessed am I, for you to be reading this, my friend.

May you prosper in all areas of your existence.

Sat Nam my friend, Sat Nam.

For Sat Purusha

"*H*ave I told you lately …

… how much your book inspires me?"

As I sit in the glow of those most beautiful of words, I realized, I truly am the wealthiest of all beings – for I have the best of friends! May we again sit together upon the mountain of Truth.

Sat Nam Ji.

Of the numbers

*C*alendar 08/08/08, how symmetrical, how, Infinite.

Just like life.

They that lived it

Who would know, but they that lived it?

In what way can we uplift and inspire this world?

Would never have thought, I'd be a writer… yet here we sit my friend….

Who could speak of what inspires each life, but they that lived it?

May we all find what inspires us.

Sat Nam.

Follow your dreams

They that lived, they that followed their dreams, they that walked into the light….

Choices, mindset, faith, hope, moments frozen for all eternity….

Nothing is ever as it seems, live, and experience it.

Step into the light and follow your dreams, I'll see you there!

Live it

There's nothing to, "Find," you already have it, be it love, prosperity or even enlightenment. Realize it and live it.

Sat Nam.

Live

You name it, worry will push it all away… Love yourself, love your neighbor, forgive, and live.

Realizations

All a prosperity meditation does is put you in touch with the wealth you already have.

Like love or anything else it's not something you find, it's something you realize you had all along.

Sat Nam.

Every step of the way

Dear friend, went through a difficult time, said I was there, holding her hand the whole time... yet physically, she's thousands of miles away....

It was then that I realized, I carry my friends with me, always....

Today we went to the Botanical Garden, I hope you all enjoyed it as much as I did. From the feeding the fish to smelling the flowers and playing in the fountains, you were with me, every step of the way....

Sat Nam Ji.

In the now

Friend once commented how he was looking forward to seeing the world through my eyes...

Almost time for another notebook....

Memories, of times both great and sad, all in the past... life is here, life is now, the future brings what it may.

Live in the now and let the universe sort everything else out.

Sat Nam.

Fairy tales

Thoughts, of pen and paper, of golden light, of words flowing across the pages of life….

Sleep beckons, what dreams await!

Walk with me

"I love and follow your work… Thank you for bringing so much healing light to our world. Sat Nam,

Gurumeet Kaur Khalsa."

Dreams of mountaintop light and moonlight nights, may I ever inspire this world, into the light.

Arya

Pure of heart, forged of the light….

How we live, of the right, unconditional love for all….

What more words might I speak, to heal this world?

May tomorrow see us together again, my friends of the light.

Sat Nam.

Baby steps

I couldn't run, I couldn't walk, but I could crawl. Hardly seemed dignifying, but after the initial paralysis any motion was a major achievement.

Mind and body agreed that the pain was excruciating, but I am not my body, I am energy, I am the Light!

How do you injure light?

This is mine

*W*e each bring the light in our own way….

Seated before a gong – mallet in hand – Devinder Kaur and the universe create the most sacred of sounds – the vibration of the Infinite itself.

Sat Nam my friends, Sat Nam.

For Crichton

*T*he universe is your playground – dance, live, be.

What happier time than this one?

What greater experience than **NOW**?

This life is your playground – enjoy it!

Peace

*I*t was with great delight I discovered one could in fact chant their cares away, in essence giving it all to the universe.

Peace was but a few quick, "Dukh Par Har Sukh Ghar Le Jaae's," away....

In the morn

*S*potted fawn crossed my path, out with its family it was....

May you live free little one, may you grow and run, may warmth find you, and may you be.

Sat Nam.

To the light

I sat down at the bright center of the universe and basked in the glow of my new friend, grateful and thankful, that the universe **always** brings us what we need, not necessarily what we want.

Here's to the light.

Sat Nam.

That's life

*T*ruer words were never spoken....

The universe never gives up, never stops growing, never stops going, so why would you?

Ek Ong Kaar – we and God are one – We are the universe, We are Infinite.

Soar

*H*ow very curious, to be able to point to a calendar and say, "Right there, that's when everything changed, that's when the entire universe stood on it's end and completely re-arranged the Infinite expanse of creation that is my existence. There, right there."

The falcon wasn't a herald, it soared in celebration of this most glorious of days, let's all soar with it!

Sat Nam my friends of the light, Sat Nam.

Write it

A great spigot of prosperity appeared – as if by magic.

Infinite hands turned the handle and abundance issued forth in great torrents – exactly as I'd written!

Now, if I can do that with prosperity, I can do the exact same thing with healing, I just need to find the words and write it upon the pages of my life….

Sat Nam.

The River of Truth

Golden river of light washed away the pain….

Infinite

Cool, rainy eve, and I wonder, of the man who lives under the highway… did he get the roof fixed?

Tiny building, next to the overpass… I wonder how Rico is….

Perspective is everything, may yours be Infinite.

Sat Nam.

Knots of life

Dis-cord, a knot in the cords of life… Bound Lotus unties them….

Find what works for you and untie the knots of your life.

Sat Nam.

Harmonics

Not surprisingly, there's a mantra for every occasion, in this science of the Light.

All harmonize your frequency with that of the Infinite.

May your existence be a harmonious one!

Sat Nam.

For Sirisimran

To again walk, free of pain – an absolute miracle! Wahe Guru!

Sirisimran, you truly are the angel of Healing, I am eternally grateful!!!

Eyes wide open

Gracious to all, no enemies will you have, neither in your heart, nor among the Infinite.

Sat Nam.

For Carwood

May the sisters of eternal light ever sing for you and yours, may the light ever shine upon us all....

May Infinity be yours, and ours....

May we learn, peace, may we all find the path to Ek Ong Kaar and see the God in all, may we all dwell in the light....

Sat Nam.

Walk with me

I'd shared a sneak preview with an angel… she replied:

"Wow Akal Sahai – the quote from "Into the light" is so beautiful!

I can't wait to read more.

Be well,

Devinder Kaur"

I basked in the glow of her divine praise, eternally grateful for all that I am and secure in the faith that, the Infinite watches over us all, as we step into the light.

Walk with me.

Be the pen

*M*y pen seemed sad as we sat down to write….

"Yeah, Notes is almost out of pages."

"I know, two more. But he was with us on the journey home and he was there when we stepped into the light."

sigh

"Besides, you called our last notebook 'Notes.'"

"That's right! Wahe Guru, Wahe Guru!"

My pen danced all day, expressing itself in Infinite ways, again vowing to, *"Change the world!"*

Be the pen.

Sat Nam.

10 Days

*R*elaxed now, pen flowed, excited about the future….

"I know! We have the date!"

"September 17th."

"What do you think will happen?!"

"Everything will change."

"I can't wait!"

Change – of that you can be certain.

Sat Nam.

Lines of confluence

*P*rosperity, Day 49….

Left the details to the universe – the fun lay in seeing how it all comes together – the myriad threads the universe weaves together to create this tapestry that is my existence.

May your tapestry be a beautiful one!

Sat Nam

Let's find out

Curiosity piqued as my appointment with destiny neared… back healing, prosperity dawning, freedom approaching – Wahe Guru!

What might lay up the road?

Let's find out!

The mantis

Sand flows through the hourglass… though I imagine the universe has little need for the concept of time….

We however do, for our time upon this plane is brief, but a blink of an eye to the Infinite….

As I sat, reading Japji, I noticed a mantis, praying as it clung to the window screen….

Just like the mantis, the universe prays, for us all, pulls for us, is there for us in all that we do. After all, you want yourself to succeed don't you?

Sat Nam

Soar and triumph!

*C*ool night and I finally feel free of the past and all that sought to hold me back….

The future unfolds with each breath, within us, the Infinite capacity to triumph over any circumstance.

Breathe deep and soar!

Relax

*R*est my angel, wings of golden light

Watch over you I will, this starry night

Even angels need to sleep sometime

Relax and leave the details to the universe

Sat Nam.

Touch of the light

Cold wind tears at the edge of night.

Suddenly I was 7 years old again, tasting my first experience of the universe at large… my first touch of the light….

The magic lives on in us all.

Sat Nam.

Answers in the night

Paths, journeys, destinations, lighthouses, pain, healing, stress, freedom, liberation, victory, answers, questions….

I guess the question is – I already know the answer before I even write the question – "How do I free myself of this pain?

Relax

Relax and rest well my friends.

Sat Nam.

Eternal Peace

No one "wins" a war, everybody loses….

Relief

Still as the night… the pain evaporated… as if it were simply switched off.

I am Infinitely grateful, not only for my healing but for *everything* – my health, my family, friends, for all that I have, am, and will ever be!

Let gratitude be the measure of a man and see what the Age of Aquarius brings us!

Wahe Guru!

Victory

Warm breeze sends the trees to and fro… storms on the way… and the words of Guru Gobind Singh fill the air…

"Chatara chakara vartee, chatara chakara bhugatay

Suymubhav subhang sarab daa sarab jugtay

Dukaalang pranaasee dayaalang saroopay

Sadaa ung sungay abhangang bibhootay."

May his words carry you to victory over all that life may bring you!

Sat Nam

Where it begins

Words of a dear friend echo throughout my being, as I stand at the precipice of change....

"You're going to be famous, you know that don't you?" Sat Purusha stated, matter of factly, as if she said, "I like rain."

What I do know is, this is the moment everything changes.

Take that step with me.

Angels of the light

Another mantis came, to pray for me, to help me realize, to help me focus on myself, not what others might or might not do... face the consequences of their actions they will.

Safe travels my winged friend....

II

The angel of Prayer stayed outside my window....

She wanted to do some Bound Lotus with me, she wanted to surrender. I wonder what burden she carries....

As we surrendered to the light she explained, "You ARE the light, leave ALL the details to the universe."

III

Something deep inside my being relaxed and at long last I experienced true healing….

Yoga's not about what position you can torque your body into, it's about relaxing – *everything*.

IV

I sat up and she was gone… as I looked about she exclaimed, *"Already know, that which you require, to complete your journey, into the light."*

Sat Nam.

"Sat Nam."

V

And so I truly relaxed, for the first time in millennium, healed, free, loved, a smile on my face….

VI

*T*hank you universe, thank you for my healing, thank you for this miracle of light.

Sat Nam

Of legacies and light

*W*e are the custodians of this world, how well have we done by it?

What world the future inherits is up to us….

One more

*N*ine more lines… how might we use them to make this world a better place? How might we help them free their minds and realize it's time to stop running?

Smile and the universe smiles with you ☺

May you always walk in the light, may the long time sun ever smile upon you and may you always have 2 more lines in the notebook of your life.

Sat Nam.

Dear Universe

*M*ay my brother rest well this eve….

In the mountains

*P*ain delivers perspective… had never fully appreciated how
   good I truly have it…

To sleep indoors, warm and dry –

To take the stairs –

To have fresh water –

To eat thrice daily –

To have the entire universe but a single click away –

To have the long time sun smile **FOR** me….

Infinite blessings my friends!

Sat Nam.

Move!

And as I floated across the plains of the Serengeti, soared above the highest mountain peaks and down the tallest of waterfalls… I… I was finally out of my own way.

The only thing in your way is **YOU**!

Now **MOVE**!

Heroes of the light

Of heroes, angels and eagles, rest well my friends, I'll watch over you this night.

Paradise

Love and live… it's the moments we carry to the other side, not the maya, what does *it* matter?

It's all just energy for the experience, live it!

Sat Nam.

Colors in the air

*A*ir turns crisp, leaves, a golden brown… autumn approacheth, I wonder what it brings….

The question

*A*t times life itself seems to derail, but how real is this life?

I mean, I can see my hand, but if my entire existence is energy, then how real is my hand and what am I to learn by the experience, other than not to think about it so much?

The answer

I am my body, won't always be, but I am now.

In the moment

What then, if now is the only moment?

Now always is, even when we experience then it becomes now.

Here and now

Outside of the body, time would have no meaning –

– and why am I thinking about this –

"This is meaning of life stuff!" my pen and notebook exclaim in unison… best of friends they already are. How well they work together!

Infinite perspective

Strange things happen and I wonder of the varying perspective, from this mortal life to an angelic one….

To observe the birth of a sun, versus watching the sun rise… to swim in the ocean or drift about in space as pure consciousness….

Mysteries of existence

Physical needs, sustenance, income, joy… I know I came to this world to evolve and perhaps make it a better place, but I wonder why I chose this world….

Infinitely

To live as a human….

By definition, life on other worlds would have to be different. There are things we just don't need to know yet – like the future.

May the "now" of your existence be bountiful, blissful, and beautiful.

Sat Nam.

The pages of life

"Do you believe we wrote that?"

The words appear in my head, the pen moves of its own accord and there it is on the page.

"Doesn't that just totally blow you away?"

pause

Given the questions I just asked – and answered – you would think so.

"But it seems very straightforward."

Sat Nam.

"Sat Nam."

More

What more riddles of life shall we ponder this eve?

So deep of thought, in motion it all is, unlock the answers in time you shall....

For Sahaj Singh

I sit, pen in hand, thinking about my brother, who was stabbed in the throat....

If I live until the end of time I may never know what to say, beyond, "get well soon brother."

Sat Nam.

In my prayers

Gives perspective, how insignificant my so called "problems" are.

Not the who, the what, or the why – it happened – and someone I may never meet is laying in the hospital because of it, stabbed in front of his family, in his own driveway….

Universe, please watch over Sahaj Singh and his family.

For Amanda

I sat, pen in hand, wanting to write something for a friend in need, something deeply moving to carry her through these tough times in which she travels, but I realized, the best thing you can ever do for a friend in need is just be there for them…

… to share a laugh, go for a hike, play a little Frisbee, to listen, but most of all, to be there for them.

I'll always be there for you.

Sat Nam.

Of riddles and light

What words would I write, what words would I speak, were the pen to find the page.

Of deeds, not wrongs, of light not dark, of riddles in the night.

Of friends, of freedom in a world gone mad.

It begins with the light….

Sat Nam.

Rivers of light

Mystifying, the myriad lines of confluence that bring our existence together, the divine interplay of creation at work….

It's a Wonderful Light

You are now in Bedford Falls….

To the richest man in town, George Bailey….

Storybook romance, friend to everyone in town, made a difference in **EVERY** life, lighthouse… couldn't see his own light….

If you had that one wish, what would it be?

May all your wishes come true.

Sat Nam.

Blessings

*R*ealized today, how cool it is to be me….

I didn't care about the credit card bills I couldn't pay, it was the lives I'd touched, just like George Bailey's realization.

Maybe I will run for President! I could form the lighthouse party… and teach the world to say, "Sat Nam."

What do you think?

Happy Birthday Ji!

I think, I know, my back's healing….

On this day of Guru Ram Das' birth, I'd said I was going to ask for 3 miracles, yet spoke not 1… why….

The Lord of Miracles would deliver, yet who was I to ask?

I am the lighthouse, that's who!

Yet I dared not ask, for anything, knowing, he would deliver what I **needed**, not what I **wanted**.

Sat Nam Ji, and Happy Birthday!!!

Of lists and angels

*D*id I dare write it? If I write it, live it I shall….

Did I dare to dream of the angel of Love?

Or of prosperity or health? Was not 3 miracles as easy as 1?

Physical pain, I'd discovered, was about opening the heart, it was Guru Prem's, *"Divine Alignment."*

Which left 2… but a single thought away.

May we all find it.

Round the corner

*W*as likely far closer than I realized, just round the corner as it were….

Everything, nothing

*I*nfinite peace, as I stepped into the moment and flew with angels, awash in divine grace….

All of my dreams were coming true at once, the moment I stopped and became… nothing.

For an angel

"This is beyond words for me," divine praise from an angel, may she fly my way again, may she shine upon us all, may her Infinite grace bless us all.

Sat Nam.

Vision of the future

I had an epiphany this morn....

In the Age of Aquarius, wealth will be measured by consciousness, friends, and the lives one touched, not by stacks of nickels....

I'll see you there.

Sat Nam.

Where energy goes

Stop, and energy flows, heals....

Pen flows across the page, creation....

Miracle is on its way, leave the details to the universe to the Infinite and rest well my friend, rest well.

Sat Nam

What words could I write that would change the world, bring peace, love, harmony and touch every soul?

Sat Nam.

Answers

Who lived it, who decided, who made it, who did it, when, where? Endless questions…

Stop, and let the answers catch up with you!

Sat Nam.

On the 16th

What would I, what could I say that would make a difference in the life of another?

Sat Nam.

Before the dawn

*B*ound Lotus, Day 1129….

Everything stops as you surrender to the Infinite, bask in the experience.

Diamonds in the rough

*I*t occurred to me, that, the cusp of the Age of Aquarius is a crucible of tremendous pressure.

We can either become diamonds or be crushed into dust, hence the world gone mad….

We're all just diamonds in the rough….

Sat Nam.

Infinite peace

*M*ind stopped, energy flowed as I basked in the glow of the angel of Peace….

What words could express the myriad of sensations, the energy, warmth, happiness and peace that coursed throughout my existence….

Caribbean Breeze

No footprints but your own upon the path of life… no directions, save one, *"Forward."*

To return to where it all began, to come full circle as it were and revisit my first writings… where the journey truly began….

Where your journey ends or begins matters not, it's how you live the moments in between.

May you live well.

Sat Nam.

Invitation to soar

I'm going to float off the planet, will you come with me?

Take my hand….

Divine love

Much to my delight, she extended her hand and together we floated right off into space, swam in the Infinite Sea and soared above the all.

Blessed by the light

*H*er angelic praise filled my being, Infinite energy coursed throughout my body, I am the lighthouse.

What words to express divine love, Infinite blessings and eternal light?

May I spend all eternity in the space where I first heard her voice....

Sat Nam.

Where the light dawns

I know what is happening, what is set in motion, what this means, where the light dawns....

Miracles of life

*T*hird miracle, lay just round the corner... no attachments to details, just a knowing.

Here's to prosperity, may it find us all!

Field of dreams

*I*nfinite love, peace and blessings to all. May the angel of Peace touch your lives as she has mine.

We'll see you on the journey.

Sat Nam.

The Golden Triangle

I'm going to float away on a cloud. Won't you come with me?

"Yes."

To peace

I'm going angel watching, wanna come?

Wish upon a star

Pen, notebook and I pondered how to express the multitude of feelings for the angel of Peace and all our brothers and sisters, of Infinite Truth, divine understanding and living the penultimate fairy tale….

"I think she'll like it!" my pen said excitedly as it began to dance and sing, "Wahe Guru! Wahe Guru!"

Peace….

I am with you

I love us more, there is no me, no you, only us… Ek Ong Kaar….

"Until we draw our last breath upon this world," said the angel of Peace as we became one being.

Dreams really do come true, but first you have to have them.

Sat Nam.

Love poems

Love, Day 6….

Infinite beauty, grace, peace and love….

I will love you until the end of time Ji.

Love letters

Divine love burst within my being with the force of 12 suns going supernova as the angel of Love showered my her love upon me.

May we all be touched by the light and angels alike.

Sat Nam.

Lover's whisper

The angel of Peace, the angel of Love, divine descriptives for the woman of my highest dreams….

Infinite gratitude

Thank you Universe for my sadhana, for my flexibility of mind, body and spirit, for my Infinite blessings, and most of all, thank you for the unparalleled majesty that is the angel of Love.

I truly am the most blessed of all creatures.

In gratitude,

Akal Sahai Singh

Raise the bar

Divine purity, Infinite grace, eternal and unconditional love, unwavering faith and a conscious life.

Raise the bar and be the lighthouse.

Sat Nam.

On the move

Hours pass in the blink of an eye, minutes linger for hours, energy on the move….

Born into the light, what words could describe the penultimate fairy tale, the dawn, divine love, purity of heart and being?

How would I tell the world, how would I tell an angel how much I love her… I'd do like George Bailey and lasso the Moon for her, that's what I'll do!!!

Morning metaphorics

Be the lighthouse so everyone can sail beyond the edges of the map and transcend the physical.

Faith and love, born of the light….

Dis-ease, burned away by the light….

Step into the light.

Sat Nam.

Keep up

Unto the ends of the Earth and beyond, unto the light....

For my Babyji

Pen paused from dancing about the house and singing, "Wahe Guru! Wahe Guru!" to sit with us....

"I've figured it all out!" My pen exclaimed excitedly. "Prosperity is the meaning of life! Think about it – the universe itself is constantly expanding, life multiplies and grows, energy expands and flows, the light uplifts. Spiritual growth, expansion, love, healing – it all relates to prosperity!"

As my pen resumed dancing and singing my notebook added, "He's never going to stop now, you know that don't you?"

laughter

Would you be able to rest if you'd just uncovered the meaning of life?

"I guess not."

"Wahe Guru! Wahe Guru!"

I know

"*Faith comes not from details.*" I know.

"*Faith comes from patience, trust and detachment.*" I know.

"*What else do you know?*" I know I love my Babyji, and that I am the most blessed and prosperous of all. Thank you universe.

"*Sat Nam.*"

Sat Nam.

I am the lighthouse

"*Do you trust me?*" Yes.

"*How far will you carry the bucket of water?*" Until everyone can drink.

"*How far will you shine?*" Until everyone can see.

"*Why?*" This is what I came here to do, to be the lighthouse.

"*Bless you. Now open your eyes and prosper.*"

Sat Nam.

Shine bright

To think, that I inspire an angel….

Flesh is transitional, I am not this body, nor is it me, yet here we are….

Lone star drifted across the sky, universe pointing the way home….

"You're the angel of Miracles," spoke the angel of Love, my babyji… I think, I'll float off into the cosmos now… see you there!

Goodnight

"*She loves me! She loves me!*" my pen exclaimed, jumping up and down.

Much more subdued, my notebook responded, "*There he goes again….*"

"*Come on Notes!!*"

It's getting late you two….

"*Oh! Oh! We see how it is, you just wanna lay us on the cold floor again!*"

"*Put us by the window.*"

Umm, it's dark outside.

"*So!*"

And here I am debating with a notebook and a pen.

laughter

Goodnight you two.

"Goodnight!!"

"No put us closer!"

sigh

One voice

"Now you know why we wanted to sit here."

It's beautiful, the fall colors, blowing about in the breeze….

"Where's our babyji?"

Healing people.

"Mmmm."

Yeah.

We speak with one voice, it's name is Truth.

Sat Nam.

Answer yes

Edges of sleep creep in as I ponder the light….

When you leave this mortal realm and the question is asked, "Did I uplift enough?" what will your answer be?

Step into the light, raise the bar and answer yes.

Miracles in the night

I thirsted and an angel let me drink the dew from her hand….

Stop by our house at 11 Wahe Guru Way and we'll do some yoga. Just come on in, the door's open.

We'll see you there….

Questions of love

"*W*hy me?" asked an angel in the night….

Why not you?

Why anyone else?

Drink now

*A*gain I thirsted and the angel returned, cupped her hands and said, "Drink now and never taste need again."

Details

At last I understood… all one really need do, is do the work, the universe will take care of everything else.

Details are the domain of the Infinite; Love and Truth a fountain from which all flows forth, the beauty of divine simplicity.

Sat Nam.

Become the light

"Tis but the beginning," an angel said as she coalesced out of the mist, "energy builds, washing away all that you were, as you become the light."

Grow with it

Awash in prosperity as I became the light….

Our souls became one as we merged with the Infinite, immersed in our abundant existence….

Light expands, grow with it.

Sat Nam.

Prophecies in the night

" **P**ut us on the couch! *"It's cold on the floor!"* my notebook and pen exclaimed as we retired for the eve.

Sure thing guys.

"Relax brother, your third miracle is here."

Just wish I knew where here was.

"Hold out your hand."

Peace and blessings

It's your thoughts, words and feelings about prosperity that determines the timeline – the universe wants you to prosper – in all areas of your existence.

Epiphanies of light

Free at last, free at last, praise be almighty, I'm free at last!

The old, blown away, to make room for the new, just like I'd written it….

Time between conception and inception vanishes as one becomes aware of the process.

Here's to the now, live it – FREE!

Taste the rainbow

Notebook, pen and I danced around the house, tasting pure delight as Infinite blessings showered upon us.

"Here comes that 3rd miracle!" my pen proclaimed as we continued our dance. "Wahe Guru! Wahe Guru!"

Taste the rainbow and live!

Carry the water

Simply put, you do the work and the universe sorts it all out.

Give want to the Infinite and be blessed.

Be the lighthouse, hold the space, and all your needs become pre-fulfilled before you ever know you have them.

I'll see you in the light.

Sat Nam.

Infinite transformation

'Twas as if a great spigot turned itself on as I became unstuck....

Elevated beyond descriptives, I became pure energy and flowed, pulsing with the Infinite vibration, everything stopped and I became the light.

I'll see you there.

Chopping wood

*L*ikely no greater gift I can give you, this window into my soul....

I have some wood to chop, I'll see you in the light.

Sat Nam

Angel of Love

"*I* let go of doubt on Tuesday, when I fell in love with you fully," an angel's Truth....

Soft breeze carried 3 words, "I love you," to keep me warm for all eternity, to light my way.

Whatever your way might be, may you find it and live, free.

Sat Nam.

Sing it

*H*eart pounding, I realized, love is the song of the Infinite….

At last I discovered what strength is, from the inside, it's when you KNOW, it's when you DO, it's when you ARE.

Love is the song of the Infinite – sing it and live!

Sat Nam.

1001

"*W*e wanna sit on the bed!*" my pen and notebook exuberantly proclaimed, far more sentient than I'd imagined….

"Many things are far more than they seem… what are goals without following the intuition to achieve them?"

Empty.

"Right!"

Hmmm.

"Now you know why, now you know how, you hopped like a frog one thousand and one times today."

Quite prescient for a notebook and pen.

"Wahe Guru! Wahe Guru!"

Follow it

One of the greatest keys of life – following your intuition – however small it might seem, the universe is guiding you.

Follow it and we'll see you in the light.

Sat Nam.

Adjectives of light

Developing, listening, waiting patiently, being in the stillness, stopping and surrendering, serving, honoring and respecting, being, living in the now, keeping up, loving, shining, blessing….

Thank you for helping to make this world a better place.

Sat Nam.

Dance in the light

Life is forward, life is now. Yes it happened, but that was then, this is now, life is now.

Realized it was time to find out who I really was… and see how long my hair wants to be….

Live in the now and dance in the light.

Sat Nam.

Blanket of love

Cradled in a warm blanket of love, an angel's love, I set out to make this day my own, to prosper, to love and to be the lighthouse.

I'll see you in the light.

Sat Nam.

Inspire the angels

The wheel of karma stopped as the floodgates opened and prosperity poured into our lives….

Angels, inspired by our work, shine for us, cheer for us, urging us on to ever greater heights.

Be the lighthouse and inspire the angels.

Sat Nam.

Working in the light

It dawned on me that all these years I've been writing, I've been working, I've been carrying the water.

All this yoga and meditation… I've been working… chopping wood….

I love you!

$\mathcal{A}$nd so I set out to create the penultimate love poem, one that shouted out to the entire universe, "I love you!"

The sun and stars shine for me, the rain, divine energy by which I grow.

Might just sing and dance 'round the house all day long!

"Wahe Guru! Wahe Guru!"

Have them

$\mathcal{D}$reams do come true, first you have to have them, then, you leave all the details to the universe and simply carry the water and chop the wood.

All things will come to you if you but do the work and have faith.

I'll see you in the light.

Sat Nam.

Keys of life

$\mathcal{F}$ocus, the key to manifesting.

Commitment, the key to success.

Faith and surrender, the keys to freedom.

Love, the key to it all….

Riders of the light

All aboard the prosperity train!

New story starts to push itself out, life wanting to be re-written in the light….

Angels, evolve with us, cry and rejoice for us, urging us into the light….

Life, *IS* eternal.

I'll see you in the light.

Manifesting the light

The light as my friend, the Word as my guide….

The Age of Aquarius is about working for everyone.

How we walk determines the journey, details are the domain of the Infinite….

Walk with me, into the light.

Sat Nam.

WOOOHOOO!

An angel stopped under the mistletoe and smiled as she pointed up.

WOOOHOOO!

May your life be filled with WOOOHOOO!

No limits

There's a blind man who works out at the gym I go to, **knows** his way around the entire building.

The only limits in this universe are the ones we place upon ourselves.

I'll see you there

Realized, this sunny, crisp morn, that the universe hadn't just brought me an angel, I'd been blessed with the love of the Goddess of Light.

I stepped into the light, into a higher dimension, one beyond the physical and basked in Infinite love.

I'll see you there.

It's up to you

The only distance is in your mind....

Is the water cold or is the mind cold?

Is it easy or is it hard?

It's up to you.

Wishing well

Here's to happy endings, love and lighthouses....

Angel brought me before an Infinite wishing well, gave me 3 coins to boot....

What would you wish for?

Science of manifestation

Beard and hair grow long as I ponder prosperity....

Meditation and mantra change your vibration to that of your goal thus bringing it to you. The space you hold determines the timeline.

Feel good, be positive, and manifest in an instant!

Carried by the light

I have a date with an angel….

Energy builds in the stillness… cool rain falls from the night sky….

We're going hiking….

Out of the darkness

*D*ay of thanks approaches, lot to be grateful for….

'Tis said it is darkest just before the dawn… that's what a lighthouse is for….

May we all find our way through the dark and into the light.

Sat Nam.

Time to fly

*A*ngel appeared beside me, wrapped her golden wings around me and said, "Rest, I'll watch over you this night."

When I woke, she was gone, one of her golden feathers lay beside me….

Within each life, there's a time to laugh and a time to cry, a time to fly and a time to embrace immortality.

It's time to fly!

Lighthouse news

*I*njuries both old and new fade in the light....

Realization dawns in the stillness....

Energy is life – focus and live!

Starting over

*T*he journey never ends and sometimes it leads us back to where we started, so we set off with a new perspective and work that much harder. Or maybe to be more present, or thankful, or any one of a million billion reasons....

The why matters not because life is about starting over and becoming more.

I'll see you in the light.

Sat Nam.

Notebook, notebook

Realized, it's not what you know it's how you know it – from the inside – that matters.

I've got a letter for you:

"I love you –

God."

Sat Nam.

Little things

Would you live for the light?

Quit worrying about the little things and live, because that's all they are – little things.

First snow

Beard grows long as light falls from the sky.

Hair is a meditation, a cold shower is a meditation, as is everything else in this realm.

Sat Nam.

Palace of light

What is triumph without adversity?

Star hung outside my window… watched it rise unto the light….

Thank you for walking with me my friend.

Lotus rising

Chose healing, chose prosperity, chose love and there it all was.

Your dreams are there, all you have to do is choose them.

Whether you seek to inspire angels, to live free and happy, to help, or even simply to be, it's all there for the choosing.

Choose the light and rise out of the water like the lotus.

Sat Nam.

Freedom

Don't remember ever being this comfortable, this happy and free….

Realized, that freedom comes through restriction and surrender – to the posture and the universe – that's the escape from the prison of the mind!

Power

Every thought sends Infinite ripples out into the universe, creating our future, our now.

Words carry Infinite weight....

Do this one thing for me please, stop and ask yourself, "What am I creating right now?"

In the rose garden

Snowed again, the angels had another pillow fight....

A star is born and the light rains down upon us in the rose garden of life....

Time to pull some weeds.

Sat Nam.

Thank you

Present, conscious, loving and living, focused and aware, being the light....

Take control of your mind and manifest in an instant!

The question you have to ask yourself is, whose mind is it anyway?

Rebirth

Returned to the proverbial precipice of life, no more metaphors, it's time to fly!

Enlightenment dawned as I chose the light and dropped the maya, i.e. the physical trappings of this realm.

Shooting star

The energy we attach to things shapes the outcome.

Words, thoughts, deeds, the space we hold, energy that attaches to the things in our lives.

It can weigh you down, or it can free you.

December 7th

Sacrifice, honor, the courage to uphold the light, to take the road less traveled and make the world a better place.

Here's to peace.

Sat Nam.

Let's do this

I am the Light.

I am the Wind.

I am the Word.

I am Change.

I am, I am.

The choice is yours.

Now dive into the light and let's do this.

Lotus of life

*L*ife blossoms when you water it with light.

Metaphors without end, eternal life, Infinite light….
Dream and live!

Land of dreams

"*C*onquer the mind and conquer the world."

Truth. Light. Peace.

What more can I say?

Do it and live it. Keep up. Be.

How to convey shifts of space, perspective and energy?

Higher.

What to speak of the light?

More.

What to do?

Shine.

What of income?

Energy.

What of the light?

Dive into it.

I'll see you on the other side.

Sat Nam.

Wake up

Sonnets of love, light and inspiration….

Shine, in service to the light.

Breathe to life, shine to grow.

What else was there to say, I'd found the woman of my dreams….

Light.

I once dreamt I woke up on the 3rd day. Let's wake up now and let's do this.

Sweet dreams

*N*irvana, liberation, Samadhi, jivan mukht, enlightenment, Universal Consciousness, Infinite awareness....

If you can dream it you can live it.

I'm dreaming of the light.

Goodnight.

In your dreams

*C*losed my eyes… was I dreaming?

Opened my eyes and there she stood – the Goddess of Love – the woman of my dreams.

Dreams do come true **IF** you have them.

Sat Nam.

Capture the magic

*W*here does the wind live?

I journeyed to the far corners of the universe and found not the source of the wind, but myself.

The wind is free and so are you.

Sat Nam.

Before the light

I was lost and then the way found me, the living Word delivered me into the Light.

The road leads into the light, all you have to do is follow it.

Sat Nam.

The way

*N*eed not see the light, need not see the way, to know it's there….

"I've got it covered," said the living Word as it filled my being with faith….

Step into the light and teach wherever you walk.

Sat Nam.

Step into it

*R*ealized the symmetry, beauty and perfection of the circle of light…

Be the Lighthouse – shine

The Journey Home – the journey into the light

Into the Light – enlightenment. Step into it.

WOO WOO!!!

*G*et ready to move, here comes the light!

Opportunities rise out of the light.

Faith grows from the light.

I'll see you there!

The conductor

*A*LLLL ABOARDDDD the prosperity train!

Your moment in the sun is now.

ALLLL ABOARDDDDDD!!

Ding ding

*R*ealized it was my thoughts about money that kept me from the Light.

Everything that I have, everything that I am – I gave it all to the light – and that's when ___________.

All you have to do is fill in the blank.

Sat Nam.

Moving forward

*I*s the journey symbolic, mental, physical, energetic or otherwise?

Life is in the here and now, a physical reality.

Left insecurity laying by the side of the road….

I'll see you in the light, come on, let's get there together.

Sat Nam.

See you there

I was born in the light, life is about finding your way home.

See you there.

Sat Nam.

Winter's Eve

*P*ressure builds, time to raise the bar.

It's about getting there – wherever there might be.

It's there

*N*eed not know the way, need not even see the light, need just know it's there.

Faith manages.

<Click>

*L*ife exists not within a game – life IS the game… now where's that reset button?

Had enough of something? <Delete>

Want something else? <Installing>

Reboot to complete installation, Yes/No?

Load program

*C*omputer, install <Job>

Locate <Work>

[Enter] <Income>

How's yours?

Hair is consciousness.

Music is consciousness.

Food is consciousness.

Life is consciousness.

How's yours?

Well?

Sex is consciousness.

Clothing is consciousness.

Every single thing we put into, onto, or expose our body to, is consciousness.

So again I ask, how's yours?

Heroes in the night

What is a hero?

One who freely sacrifices and in that instant attains liberation from the cycle of life, birth and death.

It's that magical moment of action, to whatever result, that defines our existence.

Love and honor

Wisdom, from years past, sooths a worried soul in the night… forgotten answers….

Dear Universe,

I would like to be a writer, one who gets paid to write.

Thank you,

Akal Sahai Singh

(Steve Coffing)

Letters from space

Dear Infinite,

What words may I write this day to make the world a better place, to place peace and good will towards all in the hearts of every being?

What more can I do?

Help me please, to be the answer and not the question, to bring light to the places where there are none

Jump!

I need to let go, dive into the light and let it all happen. I don't
need to know, I need to do!

For Thao

*M*ay we all have a friend like Walt.

I would like to thank you Mr. Eastwood, there are not words to
express the depth of your impact upon my existence.

May we walk together, in the light.

Peace and blessings my friend.

Greetings

I'd really just like to shake your hand, sit a bit and ask about your
journey.

May we meet along the way....

Babyji's lullaby

Now I lay my angel down to sleep.

Rest your wings, I'll watch over you….

Until we meet again

"You're almost there," she said as we parted… though I know not where, "there," is… I'll miss you and our long talks…. Sat Nam.

Moving on

It's not about what was lost, it's about what was gained and in that, I'm the most blessed of all men.

It's for the best

It's not about me telling the universe what I think I need, it's about me being still and letting the universe guide me to what is best for me.

Faith

There is hope for us as a race, we are going to make it, Captain Sullenberger and the crew of Flight 1549 are proof of where we're headed as a society.

I'll see you in the light.

Love

I know not of the power of the pen, just that this is one way I can serve the light.

I've rarely thought about my writing, just enjoyed the process and the transformation it's brought about in me.

Whatever you wish your life to be, write it and live it you will!

Sat Nam.

Hope

May this very day be the best you have ever lived and may the next be a thousand times better!

May the long time sun ever shine upon you –

May you always find your way –

And may we meet, in the light.

Sat Nam.

Truth

*G*uru = that which brings light to the darkness.

The light of Truth, what being the lighthouse is all about – serving others – shining so they can find their way.

What more can I say?

I'll see you in the light.

Sat Nam.

Altar of Truth

*S*at Nam = Truth is my name.

What more powerful statement is there?

<RESET >

*L*ife, I realized, is like a video game – if it doesn't work out, you get to do it all over again.

Hope I get it right this time 'round.

For Tosh

Did you try or did you do?

Did you live for others or did you live for yourself?

Did you serve?

Did you take credit or did you praise others?

Did you keep up?

Well?

I 'd like to draw a smiley face on the world!

☺

For Ezra

I t's not the life you lead, it's the quality you bring to it.

May yours always be the highest.

A promise

What was lost is found....

Whatever happened, happened and all is right in the universe, I promise you my friend.

I'll see you in the light, after all, where else is there to go?

I'm listening

Realized, I need not even see my own hand before my face, I just need to do like Dr. Siri Atma says and listen to the voice of my soul.

Right here, right now

It's not about what I don't have, it's about what I do with what I **DO** have.

It's going to be okay, I promise.

Segue

If you've not had the blessing of hearing Dr. Siri Atma Singh Khalsa lecture, I highly recommend you do so.

Whether he's speaking of something mind-blowingly profound, or off on yet another segue, he speaks to my soul and I am deeply honored to hold both he and his wife Nam Kaur Khalsa as the dearest of friends.

Infinite blessings my friends,

Akal Sahai Singh

Friday the 13th

Thank you universe, for everything that has ever made me laugh, made me feel sad or in any way shape or form touched my existence.

Thank you so very much for all of the Infinite miracles of this thing called life.

Sat Nam.

Day of love

Let's make every day a day of love.

Sat Nam.

Love and live!

*T*oday is the first day of the rest of your life – live it!

For Harmanjeet Kaur

*F*riend who prays for me, a life touched by the light… shine on Harmanjeet, shine on….

Of pen and notebook

"*I* carry it with me everywhere," a friend wrote of my first book….

No higher praise, than knowing my words have touched someone.

Each poem is a signpost, a marker I left, on my journey home….

When all of the hustling and bustling stops, I sit with my friends… some days it's therapy, others, it's inspirational, but it always leads me into the light.

I'll see you there.

Sat Nam.

Forgiveness in the night

Friends called out in the night, it was time to write, it was time to forgive and let go, not just of pain, but of everything.

There are 2 things in this life, that which moves you forward and that which holds you back.

This life is yours, all you have to do is live it.

Sat Nam.

Leap of faith

Now I lay me down to sleep….

Once told someone I would give her my last breath, and I still mean it….

Friends

"You are wonderful with sooo much love in your heart."*

For years I had defined my life by what I did not have, what I was not….

If it was in my best interest, I would have _______. That's all life really is.

Thank you Sat Purusha, for your radiance, your support, and most of all, for being my friend.

Sat Nam.

In service

Watershed moment, when I realized, that through my writing, I could uplift the entire planet, that through my writing, I am serving *everyone*.

I had never truly thought about my writing, I just enjoyed the process....

In that magical moment, I was truly free, free at last, free at last.

I'll see you in the light.

Sat Nam.

Who am I?

Pen and notebook want to go with....

Hair grows long... time to find out who I really am....

Finally know what I am – a writer.

Truth is my name.

Sat Nam.

For Milton

"*Skills to pay the bills.*"

Beautiful, simply beautiful….

You work hard, you learn, apply yourself and like Milton says, "*Skills to pay the bills,*" will be yours.

Sat Nam my brother, Sat Nam.

Serve the light

"*I*'m grateful for you." Such praise from my sister of the light….

One task in this life – serve the light.

Sat Nam.

Be the lotus

Woke up one day and the Infinite vibration was all there was… all else had stopped… I had risen out of the mud and become the lotus….

Be the lotus and rise up, into the light.

Sat Nam.

To victory

No pressure in this life save that which we place upon ourselves.

Breathe and do your best.

Now, on to victory!

Awakenings

To all my friends:

Thank you for your Infinite support as I discover who and what I am.

I'll see you in the light.

Sat Nam.

"Let's go draw smiley faces on the world!" My pen exclaimed most exuberantly in betweenst dancing around the house and singing, "Wahe Guru!"

Fine line between success and failure… I figure if I can help one person find the light I will have succeeded in this life.

In service,

Akal Sahai Singh/ Steve Coffing

I am love

I am in love, that is to say, I am love….

Students and teachers, lighthouses, service and shoulders to stand on….

Not to ponder, just to note, this is where it truly begins….

Stop by and we'll do some yoga.

Sat Nam.

In service to the light

*T*hese words are me….

Friends comment, on how calm I am….

Infinite compliments, on my ever growing beard….

I am the lighthouse, unmoved, shining for all….

What higher may I share, than all that I am?

These words, are me.

Sat Nam.

11 Wahe Guru Way

These words upon these pages shall I speak….

I shall not teach you to run, I will teach you to fly!

Stop by and we'll do some yoga.

Sat Nam.

Wants and needs

What is want, but the failure to realize that the universe always provides exactly what we NEED?

What we need do most is leave the details to the Infinite.

I'm off to watch the angels gather the light for the morn. Who's coming with?

Questions in the night

Infinite echoes throughout my being as I ponder a perfectly tied turban… it's a meditation.

Into the light, into the energy, into the vibration we meld, no lines between where we end and the Infinite begins… not even dreams, just a simple question – How can I serve, how can I serve the light?

Sat Nam.

Infomercials of light

I'm a commercial for the light… or is it infomercial?

Want, need, who, external conflict – nothing – save the Infinite stillness and vibration, echoing throughout my being….

One goal, one purpose – to serve the light. What else is there?

Sat Nam.

Union

*E*verything is nothing, but then, doesn't that make it something?

Bound Lotus is just this thing I do 1/48th of my day… I sleep 1/3 of it… though sometimes I wish it was ½!

Everything just is… energy, light, life… everything is Infinite….

Sat Nam.

Safe travels

*I*n the land before time… of which I dream….

Before clocks ruled our existence, when we lived among the stars of which I dream….

If only I did dream… somewhere along the line… everything seems to have been switched off and my mind became just that – mine.

Wherever the road takes you – it is just that – yours.

Safe travels.

BE

'**T**was not always this contemplative, this meditative, was I someone else?

What stopped, what started, I remember not… words form, and I write them down….

Vibration echoes, rain falls, light shines – everything *IS*.

BE.

Arranging the light

Four deer on the run… totally made my day… amazing how the universe arranges the light….

MY mind

Guru Gobind Singh wrote, "*Ray man eh bidh jog kamao-o.*"

"Oh my mind, practice yoga in this way." What sweeter command?

Oh my mind, you are mine.

The way II

Highest goal – to serve the world – everyone – everywhere....

Universe, how do I best accomplish that?

Show me the way....

Pop!

Joints stretch, the body opens, energy on the rise....

Things happen, at times a sign to become more, to make a new choice, to expand, to set our sights a little higher, to rise, into the light.

I'll see you there.

Sat Nam.

All for one

*I*t's time to free the light!

"But I am the light!" my pen exclaims most exuberantly.

"Then free yourself," my notebook instructs… speaking for us all….

Shine

*P*erspective truly is everything….

Your entire world can change with but a tiny shift in energy, focus, or perspective.

Be the lighthouse and shine for all.

Sat Nam.

Under the lighthouse

*P*oem wants to be written… metaphors of light… under the lighthouse….

All life is a metaphor, the only question is, in this moment what can I do to serve?

May we all find our answers, under the lighthouse….

Sat Nam.

Happy Birthday

I see my brothers and sisters everywhere….

Somewhere along the way, my turban and I became one… who would have thought such a thing, from a piece of cloth….

Birthday on the morrow… what can I can do better, what more can I do?

In service,

The lighthouse

For my Mom

T o the best mom ever:

How clearly I hear Grandma's voice, "Kathleen Marie Theresa!!"

Thank you for teaching me to look both ways before I cross the street, for teaching me to skip rocks, to sing and not care how I sound, for the Infinite readings of Timmy Mouse, for sharing your love of water with me and especially for being the best mom ever!

Last but not least, thank you for sharing your love of making things grow… with these seeds may you bring much life to the sands of time.

Sat Nam.

In your heart

Appreciate what you have while you have it and it will always be yours.

All

...Scant 11 minutes of my birthday remain....

An angel wrote, "*The world is a better place with you in it,*" I am here to serve....

What might I do in this moment to make the world a better place, how can I do more, how can I serve **all**?

Universe, show me the way.

Reflections

I'm in love – with the Light – what else is there?

Sat Nam.

What am I?

*L*ove.

Energy.

Truth.

Peace.

A son.

Male.

A writer.

Free.

Infinite.

The lighthouse.

I am the answer, not the question, I am, I am.

In the mirror

I see the light… I see myself….

Always

My kingdom is here. I carry it with me, always….

For Harsimrat

"Are you the lighthouse guy?" she asked with a smile… my reputation precedes me ☺ to be recognized as the lighthouse – as the light – Wahe Guru!

For Angela

Angel resting… smiling softly as she floats along on a cloud….

Wherever the journey takes you, may your exuberance ever shine through!

Sat Nam.

Best weekend EVER!!!

I'd asked for an angel's indulgence – to hold her – I would have been thrilled with a few moments… she gave me an hour… all a part of the best weekend EVER!!!

Service

*Y*ou hold your arms up, you do, you serve, and the Infinite blesses you.

IS-NESS

*A*ngels shared their energy with the light, lighthouse shines all the brighter.

Thank you my sisters of the light for this divine understanding, this blessed union of energy, this sacredness, this IS-NESS that is all that IS!

Sacredness

Everything is sacred – touch, embrace, love, light, life, service.

What higher way to serve than to be the lighthouse?

Answers in the rain

Service.

Generosity.

Infinite energy, in the stillness.

Nothing.

Zero.

Moving without moving.

Infinite understanding.

No more questions, only service.

I'll see you in the light.

Sat Nam.

Feel it!

Free energy, Infinite energy, Divine understanding….

Ride the waves of change into the light – I'll see you there!

Into the vastness

Connection on an Infinite scale, oh what wonders await!

Into the vastness!

Ek Ong Kaar

Where I end and where the Infinite begins… vanished in the night, in the Infinite energy between us all.

I'll see you there, Sat Nam.

On the morrow

*B*est 3 days ever – EVER!!!

Sheer perfection, divine beauty and grace, I cannot wait to see what the morrow brings!

Wahe Guru!

Closed loop

*T*o serve with honor, respect and generosity.

To give, all that I am and to have it return to me a thousand fold, to have an angel visit me to exchange energy on an Infinite scale, to create a sacredness beyond words… Infinite blessings my sister.

Sat Nam.

Live it!

*T*oday is the best day EVER!!!

Rejoice!

I feel so free I could fly, dance, laugh, sing and cry all at the same time! Oh what my pen would say!

"Wahe Guru! Wahe Guru!"

And tomorrow will be even better!

Being there

*C*osmically, Infinitely vast, grander, larger than epic, beyond which the words of man can convey – be there!

All there is

*T*oday is the best day ever, I'm in love with the light!

Love, on a cosmic scale, is all there is.

Sunshine

*A*ngels invited me to come gather the light with them… we snacked on sunshine as we watched the Infinite vibration become the light… best day ever, step into it!

Kissed by the sun

I paused to bow at the feet of the Goddess and <touch> her feet… she smiled and blessed me…

To serve and to shine is all I ask.

The taxman

*O*ne day, all we'll have is Sat Nam….

Barefoot in the grass

*W*aves of undulating energy, reverberate throughout the body… Sat Nam… Sat Nam… Sat Nam… Truth on the rise….

What else is there?

Free

I'd like to spend my days barefoot, walking in the grass… the surf… the light… among the stars….

Up!

*T*ingling energy, heat, on the rise, waves of energy, pulsing, up, up, UP!

Mother's love

*R*emember when you were little and your mother held you and made everything alright?

I'd like to live in that space, no cares, no worries, just peace, love and light.

I'll see you there.

Sat Nam.

Gone with the wind!

Maple seeds tossed into the wind, each one a care that sought
to weigh me down....

One by one, they fluttered from view and were gone with the wind!

It's open

Flexibility and strength are of the mind, the body merely
follows suit....

Eagles and angels soar, dance and dream alike… free of it all.
Eagles soar and angels serve… no games, just the sky and the light.

Stop by the lighthouse at 11 Wahe Guru Way and we'll do some
yoga, just come in, it's open.

Dance!

What do dreams mean, what happens when our body and mind
go to sleep?

Does our soul get out and dance in the universe?

On my mind

Angel said I was in her dream… maybe we were gathering the light, maybe she stopped by the lighthouse to do some yoga….

How can I serve you?

Same thing

Arms… sore from repeatedly pushing myself up off the floor… or was I soaring with angels and eagles?

Same thing….

To new friends

Dove came to live on my balcony… made itself a nest on a chair….

I wonder what brought it to the lighthouse, of its travels and how it cranes its neck to look at me… safe travels my friend, you're always welcome here.

Hi!

"I'm drifting… wrapped in a blanket of your words," an angel whispered as she fell asleep….

One of the wonders of the universe – how she puts so much love and energy into a single, *"Hello."*

5 words

Realized those 3 words couples speak to each other were not adequate to express my feelings… it was then that these 5 words came to me: You and I are one.

My angel smiled and I knew she understood ☺

May you communicate well.

Sat Nam.

12 days

What would it be like to walk at the center of the universe?

We'll find out in 12 days….

Make it

...**E**specially grateful to have walked barefoot through the grass this day....

Life is what you make it, live it!

In the air

Missed the flowers entirely... how long had they been in the sunshine waiting for me to inhale their beauty?

Doesn't matter, what does, is that the hustling and bustling stopped.

Let's go see them again ☺

For Mr. Spock

Dear Universe,

I've been blessed in many ways, I ask simply to prosper.

May we all live long and prosper.

In service,

Akal Sahai Singh

(Steve Coffing)

Ishnaan

*N*eed not understand the mechanics of a stone cold shower to experience its miraculous effects upon my being… conquering the mind as the nonsense washed down the drain, Wahe Guru!

Nary a sound

*M*rs. Dove had her babies – on my balcony no less – and I didn't even know it until they'd hatched.…

I wonder of her travels and what journeys led her to a chair on my balcony to bring her young into this world.…

Sat Nam.

For Jimmy

*F*inally lived it – changes in latitude, changes in attitude. Sometimes we really do need a change of scenery.…

We will always be, by the lake sitting in the nothingness, outside the matrix, the big city off in the distance.…

I'll see you there.

Sat Nam.

For Amelia

*L*ife itself is the adventure of a lifetime – live it!

Things happen, healing and pain are all there for the experience.

I'll see you in the light. Sat Nam.

It's your move

*L*ike, that day when life suddenly came together – today's that day – step into it.

Reborn in the light

*H*ealing is a choice….

Pick up the pen and live in the light.

Life writes itself, all you have to do is live it.

Sar Nam.

Best day EVER!

Wind in your hair, sun on your face, what else is there?

Live it.

Wealth of friends

Here's to the richest man in town – George Bailey.

May we all reach such an understanding of this wonderful thing called life!

Sat Nam.

June rising

Every thought matters, every word counts, each action is your legacy.

Be, Infinite.

Sat Nam.

Where Yogis dwell

*T*hat's where I'm going – the land of the Yogis.

I imagine I'll know when I get there, see you there!
Sat Nam.

Breathe deep

*L*ife – it's all about the breath.

Breathe deep and live!

Arms up!

*Y*our focus *IS* your reality – it's as easy as you decide it is.

Stop trying to do – breathe and let the universe support you.
Now let's do some yoga!

The big jump

Baby doves, spent their entire life on my balcony… smaller one crawled to the edge, mayhap pondering the big jump….

I turned and she was gone, her bigger brother still sitting on the nest….

As she flew off I heard her exclaim, "Life's out here, live it!"

Growing pains

Time to fly… interesting that the smaller bird got it and the larger bird sat on the chair stretching its wings, hungry and alone in the dark….

Have none

Whatever you think your limit is – you're right!

I'm here to tell you, you have none, now live!

On the 6th

No, I don't need to know the future, I know the now.

Sat Nam.

The end

Sam chose to love and lived happily ever after.

May all your endings be happy ones.

Sat Nam.

Breath of life

Miracles do happen, dreams are realized every day, first you have to have them.

Have faith, keep up, ***BREATHE*** and the world will be yours!

Sat Nam.

In the night

*R*elationship: ships that relate, for varying periods of time. Warranty not included!

Sat Nam.

Of the Tarot

*M*ayhap the Fool has the most courage of all, focused only on the goal, not the journey.

Destination: The Light, enlightenment, liberation.

No barriers, no impassable chasms or trials of fire along the way, just the destination – The Light.

I'll see you there.

Sat Nam.

Laid bare

*R*ealized the only thing keeping me from my goals and dreams was me. Once I got out of my own way the Universe was laid bare before me….

May we all walk there together.

One step closer

*B*reath = life, simplest of equations, but it's also our connection to the Infinite.

Breathe deep and live!

Steps in the night

*D*epth of breath, depth of life, one step closer....

The Master's Touch

*I*t's not a question of what direction to apply effort, it's about being still and letting opportunity come, letting it find you rather than seeking it out.

Sacredness of Life

*E*very thought, every word, Infinitely precious.

Every **thing** in this life is temporary, even our time upon this realm – cherish it!

Secret of Life

*S*top chasing about and let life find **YOU!!**

Answers, not questions

*N*eed only stop asking the questions – that's when the real answers come.

Into the stillness

*N*othing to think up, need only be still and let the ideas come into the stillness.

On the 13th

*I*nto the stillness – that's where I'm going – where the angels live, where Yogis dwell… see you there!
Sat Nam.

Look up

*A*ngels gather the stars and store them in the mountains… beacons that shine through the night….

For Ellie

I wanna live now!

Maybe I'll tie balloons to my house and float to South America too!

Know thyself

*R*elationship: If you cannot relate to yourself no one else will be able to either.

Happy couple

More than anything, I think everyone wants someone to spend eternity with, life was the adventure and live they did!

May we all live like Carl and Ellie.

Sat Nam

The Ellie badge

Greatest lesson of life: Just gotta let it go – every *thing* in this realm is just that – a thing – the sooner we accept that, the sooner we free ourselves.

For Russell

Where do you park your airship?

Sometimes you just need a good cry ☺

Rewrites of life

Life's a movie, I'm re-writing the script of mine!

On the hill

Cosmic steam roller flattened the land beyond belief… to the horizon in all directions… nary a stone out of place: perfection.

Sat Nam.

Moving time

Infinite praise, Infinite blessing.

See you in the light.

Sat Nam.

And inhale!

Breath, our connection to the Infinite, what else is there?

Service.

Honor.

Love.

Sat Nam.

For Scott

Carried on the blessings of my many, many friends, I complete my journey into the light.

What a blessing, to have a complete stranger shout out, "Cool beard guy!" as I walked past….

Sat Nam.

Be yourself

Enlightenment dawned as I realized it wasn't about doing it was about being – ME.

The one thing I can do better than anyone else in existence is be me ☺

Sat Nam.

For the Doctor

*I*t wasn't about hitting my hands together, doing this or that meditation, it's all about listening to the voice of my soul.

I truly am the wealthiest being who has ever lived.

I'll see you in the light.

Sat Nam.

One step

"*H*e's single and he's divine," Such glowing praise from the dearest of friends… I feel one step closer….

21

*P*erfect day on the mountain of Truth… spent keeping up with friends.

Thank you Deva, Dyal, Nam, Siri Atma and Jasleen for the best day ever!

Sat Nam.

Reach for the rainbow

Dreams of rainbows, stars and life among the Infinite… realized I was living it.

Who could ask for anything more!

On target

Basked in divine praise, showered upon me by the dearest of people… consciousness raised to a golden light….

I'll see you there.

Sat Nam.

Dawnings

Realized who and what I truly am on the inside – Divine.

No more hustling or hassling, whatever you think is best Universe.

Sat Nam

Timelines of light

You go where the road takes you and you get there when you get there.

What am I?

The light.

On the road again

I can touch every life and that's all that matters.

Sat Nam.

Revealed by the light

Answers come to those who wait, those who breathe, those who have patience.

Step up

*T*ime comes when you either step up, or you step out. Choice is yours.

Little help here please

I think that is a parent's greatest wish for their child – a career.

Where's mine?

My time

*N*one of it matters, I am the light.

See you there

Destiny

I will always love you.

Where the river runs

There's a lighthouse at the center of the universe.

Hope to see you there!

Sat Nam.

Be, more

River runs where it will, lives and grows of its own accord – just like us.

Change our own destiny we can, the one thing we can always do in this life is be, more.

Sat Nam.

Principles of life:

1.   Meaning of life = listening to the voice of your soul

2.   Strengthening the aura and arcline facilitate #1

3.   Depth of breath = depth of life

4.   Flexibility of mind, body and spirit = adapt, improvise and accept

5.   Stillness of mind and openness of heart

6.   Serve all

7.   Forgive all

8.   Sat Nam (Truth is my name)

9.   Wahe Guru (I am in ecstasy when I experience the indescribable wisdom)

10. Ek Ong Kaar (We and God are One)

11. Be the lighthouse

Stillness of mind

Only in the stillness will you hear, will opportunity find you.

Choices in the night, guidance, direction, call it what you will, but listen and live.

Sat Nam.

Touched by the light

"I will pray so you are inspired."

Realized as I basked in the radiance of those beautiful words that as long as I have my notebook and pen I have all that I need and nothing else matters.

Writing elevates my consciousness, worry lowers it.

It's not about what I think I need it's about the pen, listening to the voice of my soul and letting it flow.

Thank you Cecilia, bless you and thank you.

Anand

Cool breeze wafts throughout my being as pen meets page in divine bliss....

Curious, to leave the computer behind and exist without thought – my mind/no mind – open.

Sat Nam.

Nests of light

Mrs. Dove returned to my balcony to again create life.

Again, 2 babies, one smaller than the other, to soon take their first steps upon this realm, fly off and create their own lives.

Safe travels.

Knights of the Light

Everything comes in the stillness, without it what is there? Worry? Questions? Seeking? Chasing?

Something turned off, some cosmic switch was flipped, all thought ceased and my mind became an empty vessel to be filled with the light of the universe.

Sat Nam.

Avalon

No more games – only light.

Shifts

Higher, more, metamorphosis of light.

Day 1.

Nothing will ever be the same, friends for all time, the light and I.

Sat Nam.

All the better

Deeper the stillness, deeper the silence the better….

Wonder if I can write my way to enlightenment… doesn't really matter, I write to serve, I write to write, I write because it is who and what I am.

Who and what are you and how satisfied are you with your answer?

Sat Nam.

Do it

What is that one thing you have dreamt of doing your entire life but have never gotten around to doing?

Do it and write and tell me how it was!

In the flow

That's where I live, stop by and we'll do some yoga.

Sat Nam.

Stretching my mind

Mayhap it was bent, or rather, I think it's supposed to be… think outside the box and all that….

After all, realized the only box is the one we put ourselves in – ie, self imposed limits.

Sat Nam.

Step lightly

Openings of light and dark, it's all in where you choose to walk.

Sat Nam.

Writing of the light

Nothing to think up, only to be.

For Sat Purusha II

May all the world know laughter such as this, how one picture can create a smile such as the world has never seen.

Depth of life, depth of beauty, may it smile upon you!

Sat Nam.

Sunglasses at night

Where is Aunt Denise and her ever present sunglasses?

Mind became mine in the stillness, scant else seems to matter… here's to whatever comes next!

Just being

No more telling the universe whatever it is I think I need, no more thinking, just being.

Sat Nam.

In good time

Most prolific day of writing in years… if I could finish this book in a day could I not attain the light or right any reverse with equal swiftness?

What's more, what does it matter?

All in good time….

New construction

Let's build on the foundation of yesterday to create a better today.

Sat Nam.

Rise up

New day, new light, rise up and meet it.

Sat Nam.

Let it flow

I didn't think about it, I just kept on writing – for myself, for everyone – it just flows through me.

Wherever life leads you, let it flow.

In step

A rms seemingly move of their own accord, in time with the breath, in time with the heartbeat of the universe.

Stay in step.

Let it be

R ealized I'd been going about it all wrong – I could never get anywhere by trying to get there.

I had to carry the water, chop the wood and let the chips fall where they may....

Switches of light

Worry keeps abundance just out of reach.

It's as easy as you make it – become too attached to the maya of this realm and forever imprison you it will.

Pitfalls of life

Maya = trappings of this physical life, trap you they will!

Flow of life

Life writes itself if you but hold the pen and let it flow.

For Sarabjot

Bound Lotus, Day 1400….

Life forms at the edge of the senses, distant wisps of the Infinite….

Beard and hair grow long, curious to see me become myself....

Fascinating to see, how we've changed these past 4 years… wonder what the next 4 years will bring....

The Light.

Sat Nam.

4 Years on

*I*t's getting on 4 years since our time together in the desert and I wonder of my brothers and sisters from the Ghost Ranch.

Marriage, divorce, children, new careers and locations I know, but most of all, I pray this finds you well.

Sat Nam.

Peace and quiet

*A*fter all these years my mind is finally just that – mine.

Beyond the stillness

"He's my friend," Cool breeze upon my face as the Infinite blessed me with these divine words, "lighthouse and beacon of strength, courage, and eternal wisdom!"

What more can I say, I truly am blessed. Thank you universe.

Sat Nam.

It just is

Need is a fear based illusion perpetuated by the ego to further its own existence.

No judgments – it just is – all things come into the stillness.

Working for the light

Aren't we all?

Peace and light

Does worry set in, does fear take root?

'Tis the question before us all.

Sat Nam.

The next thing

"*Come here,*" My notebook said to my pen and I, "*I want to write.*"

"What about?" I asked as we all sat down together.

"The light? Changing the world? Income?"

Notebook and I paused in unison to look at our pen and the first serious words it's spoken in years….

"Sleeping in the shade? Patience?"

"*No, the next thing, whatever it might be.*"

Our world

Sooner we see it as our world, the sooner we make it a better place.

Home free

I know it'll all work out – I've seen it.

All I have to do is hold that one leading thought and I'm home free.

Taste of home

N ot to try to write but to live in the space where it flows through me.

Laurels of light

O bviously cannot rest on your laurels but how do I acknowledge the enumerable deeply moving and heartfelt comments my writing has received?

How do I thank each and every person whom my words have touched?

You just did.

Sat Nam.

Be true to yourself

I'm writing this for you.

Sat Nam.

Gifts of the light

*P*lenty of pages left in the notebook of life, plenty of life left to write….

Planting the light

*W*hat it's all about – the light – serving it and spreading it.

Reality check

*C*an I write my way into the light?

Infinite brings words to life.

Ideas + energy = reality.

Illumination

Liberation from need, from fear, lack, distraction, reaction, is within all our reach.

Depth of light

The light is all around us, there is no moving closer to its source in a physical sense, we ourselves are the source of the light.

It's all about being true to ourselves and each other.

Sat Nam.

Have pen will travel

Let the breath of life move you along.

Sat Nam.

To the editor

Dear Infinite,

Thank you for my freedom, for my good health, my dear friends and family, for all things.

Bless you, thank you.

Sat Nam.

Belief system

Belief in the illusions keep me from liberation.

What need exists that is not met by the light?

It's the illusion that I do not have every thing I need in this instant that keeps me from —-

I am the light and I will outshine the illusions of this realm.

Truth is my name, wherever you see the light I am there. See me and see yourself.

Sat Nam.

Unfinished business

*I*s life truly ever complete?

Am I writing? Creating? The main thing is, I'm listening.

Some journeys take lifetimes.

If yours leads you past the lighthouse, stop in and say, "Sat Nam."

Sat Nam.

Pen calls

*L*ight calls us all home, opens our hearts and teaches us to love.

You have to put the intention out there and let the Infinite fill in the details.

That's what life is – letting go and being the lighthouse.

Sat Nam.

For everyone

*A*nyone can attain enlightenment – anyone who chooses the light over the illusions.

Baptism of light

You anoint yourself when you step into the light.

Destination

Did I dare to dream that dream?

I know I did, I'm almost there, I know it.

For Alan

Light to see by, choices we make, choices of light.

Live well.

Godspeed

Until we meet in the light.

Offerings

*L*ight – best I have to offer.

See you there.

Now what?

*L*eave it all to the light.

What else is there?

Momentum of light

*E*ver feel as if you were this far from something beyond description, like the entire universe moved in slow motion as it watched you being reborn, in the light….

Walk in the light

Distance to the light is of the mind, just have to choose to be there.

Sat Nam.

Good morning

And I woke up in the light… until then….

Be

To exist as absolutely nothing and become – everything.

Homecomings

It's not even excitement, it's a knowing. I'm going home.

See you there!

Steps of light

Certainty of purpose, certainty of light....

Distillation of light

Poems shorten, distance shortens, messages grow clearer in the light.

The easy button

Whatever it is, decide it's easy and experience that you will: "________ *is easy, let's do it now,*" and make it your reality you will.

Sat Nam.

Remembrance of light

Enlightenment isn't something you attain, it's something you remember you already have.

Trifecta of light

Universe is the light, we are the universe, we are the light.

Light travels

Flow of light, flow of life, it's already yours – realize it.

Frame of mind

Conviction of light, purpose… flexibility starts in the mind, body follows suit.
So too it is with the light.

Next

Now serving number – YOU!

Prayers of light

*B*low the cobwebs out of your life and bask in the light.

Class of light

*L*ight ~ what it's all about.

Paths of light

*I*t's where I walk.

Walk with me.

Ingredients of life

*L*ight, love, peace, honor, service, faith, courage are what you're made of.

All roads lead home, may we meet along the way.

Pages of life

This is mine, read me a page of your life.

Mantra of life

"It's easy to ________, let's do it now."

Decide it and live it you will.

Befriend the light

It's what you're made of, everything is.

The same thing

Essence of light, essence of life.

Experience of light

Change your mind and change your experience of life.

Waves of light

Ride one home.

Blessings to the Infinite

Thank you universe for all that I am, for all that I will ever be, for all things, bless you, thank you.

Homecoming

Woke up in the stillness… I'm staying ☺

Decisions, decisions

Everything we do is a choice, may you always choose well.

Flow of light

I don't try to write, it flows through me.

Don't try to live, let life flow through you.

Akal Sahai unplugged

Energy pulsing, cool breeze upon the mind, listening… away from the technology….

Unplug yourself once in a while and walk barefoot through the light….

Education of light

Distractions serve the ego….

Embrace the light and embrace life. How many more ways can I say it?

I'll keep on saying it until I uplift the entire world.

Sat Nam.

Workshop of light

Coming to your town – now.

Into the night

Let's pick up the pen and see what flows out….

Elevation

*I*t's about raising the energy, about raising the awareness….

Grace

*F*riends read my book to their classes, what a blessing, what an honor!

Treasures of light

*F*riends comment on how they can feel the energy of my book….

May the energy of your words touch all.

I've found my Treasure Island, stop by, we'll do some yoga!

Good karma

*W*hat's left when you burn away all the karma?

Let's find out!

Rise above

*D*ove sits atop the roof, warbling its plaintive tone, wonder if it'll return to my balcony to again create life….

Dreams and goals

*O*f angels, serving the all and merging with the Infinite/universal consciousness, higher experiences of the light within us all. Sat Nam.

In the now II

*P*resent tense: Is your life a metaphor of light? What would you have it be?

Euphemisms

*O*ften wondered about the metaphors of light… subject matter chooses me, just as you choose the light.

In servitude

What more is there to say about the Infinite light within you?

What more can I do to uplift the denizens of this realm, to connect them to their own divinity.

In what way can I serve?

"Remind them where they come from."

Reminders

Infinite shines through us all.

Disconnect from the illusions.

Free your mind.

What more can I say, it's time to move higher.

The next level

It's not about attaining the light, it's about connecting to the light within.

Maya

Don't exchange one distraction for another, you'll never get home.

For my Dad

I have the coolest Dad ever.

My dad is so handy I think he could build air. I mean, I can build computers, but I think, a hammer, couple of nails, and he could build air!

Has to be easier than building a house and I watched him do that when I was a kid.

I know I'm biased, I bet your family's pretty awesome too!

Skipping stones

Idyllic childhood spent roaming over hills and through streams, fishing and I'd be remiss if I did not mention my Mom who taught me how to laugh and skip rocks, took me swimming and always read to me.

May you skip through life.

Sat Nam.

Realities of life

Need to temper fantasy with reality….

Doves come and go, building a new home upon my balcony….

Enormity of task – that's in your mind, that's your ego at work.

Simplicity of life – like the doves – build a nest, gather food and fly!

See you in the sky!

Titles of light

Manifesting the light.

Caliber of light.

Governed by the light.

I'm going with it.

Weight training

Strength of mind = strength of life.

Radiance of life

*T*ruest measure of a life is by the lives we touch.

For you

*B*less you and thank you for all your support.

I'm honored to call you friend.

Sat Nam.

You're all invited

*T*o cover new ground, to journey ever higher, to stop by and do some yoga, to carry the water and chop the wood, you're all invited on this journey home.

There's nowhere else to go, that's what life is – a journey home.

Song of life

Life is a melody, what tune are you playing?

Alliterations of life

Metaphors move higher as the journey becomes clearer....

In unison

Writing and I evolve together, I write it and then I live it.

Keep on writing your life to its highest and I'll see you there.

The Light

I'm going for it, I know where my destiny lay....

Soul food

Work that feeds the soul….

Not that I've entrusted you with my soul but I have shared a lot with you. That's what life is – sharing.

Sat Nam.

Happiness

Life is **FOR** the experience, is to **BE** experienced.

You

It's all about you – this is all **FOR YOU!**

It's a mindset

Initiative, drawn into the light, called home, divinity drawn out by the light.

My friend

Notebook fills with words of light, written in praise and desire to ever deepen our relationship with the Infinite.

Monstrous ego

Demons of life, minions of the ego.

Spring cleaning

Cluttered house, sign of a cluttered mind.

Golden egg

Tiny egg appeared under Mrs. Dove this morn – life on the way!

Pool of radiance

May your life be a pool that nurtures and nourishes all.

Sat Nam.

Who am I?

Mind continues to fill with thoughts of the light:

Student of light/servant of the light – it's what I am.

We the people

We the people, in order to form a more perfect universe, hereby set forth these principles of Light:

1. Truth is my name

~ You fill in the rest ~

Highest dreams

Words of a friend echo throughout my being, "You keep going like you are and you'll be enlightened."

Hope so....

Make it so

Dear Universe,

I would like every step of my day, every breath I take to be in service to the all, to serve and spread the light.

Let's make it so.

Akal Sahai Singh

(Steve Coffing)

Cast no shadows

"*You have to keep saying it until everyone hears.*"

Sat Nam.

Expansiveness

*I*ntentions as they say are everything….

Beard continues to expand in all directions, hope my consciousness is following suit….

Worldly concerns

*L*eft all of that behind….

I am not of this world, none of its limitations apply to me – or you.

Moving higher

Teach me what lessons you will Universe,

Stream of consciousness

Hair flows free, like the mind, like the wind....

Baggage drop off

Deeper understanding, greater letting go… may they be yours....

Arrow of Truth

Fly straight.

Stagnancy of life

Get up and stir the energy around!

Physicality

All such things are temporary.

House of light

Build one.

Check out time

I'll leave when my work is finished.

Balance of life

There has to be a balance between raising the consciousness, serving, and income… may we all find it….

Sat Nam.

Evolution

Mind turned completely off….

Big bang theory

Timelines are of the mind, the Universe is of the now.

You can create anything in an instant, it's all about focus and determination.

Sadhana

Strengthening the drive, determination, resolve and faith, I think that's the true essence of what yoga does for me.

What does life do for you?

Flow

Writing flows through me like Niagara Falls, now let's create some income.

My dream job: yoga teacher and writer, but whatever you think is best universe.

To live barefoot

For years, my finances *HAD* been a black hole, let's change that right now.

I'd just like to live barefoot and serve everyone.

Sat Nam.

Miracles of creation

Writing of the light brings me to it, let's create income too....

Life of light

It's not about what I think I don't have, it's about serving and leaving the details to the Infinite.

Marching orders

Mind is mine, ego you have to go – get out – my life is mine now.

No worries mate

Worrying about it won't help, doing something about it will.

Aim high

At the very least I'm writing my way home, at the very highest I'm elevating the entire planet.

Cold showers

Conquer the cold and conquer life.

Invincible spirit

May you have one.

Pages of light

Pages of life ~ what's in yours?

Being the lighthouse

*I*t's all about the brightness ~ shine on.

Baker's dozen

*T*hings I have no further need of:

1. Ego

2. Fear/doubt/worry

3. Negativity

4. Judgment

5. Attachment

6. Want

7. Need

8. Reaction

9. Illusions

10. Competition

11. Chasing

12.

13.

Situational awareness

What can I do right now to make myself a better person, to become more?

Roll on

Chasm between the light and I vanished as I stepped within….

Irony

Maybe I'm already in the light and don't even know it yet, looking for that which I already am….

Progression of light

Chasm between want and desire vanished in the light ~ whatever you think is best Infinite.

Balance

*H*air grows long, time upon this plane shortens....

Work for it

*R*eality of life is, I need income.

Where's the balance between uplifting humanity and being able to pay my bills?

"You have to work for it."

Sat Nam.

Balance sheet

*C*an't spend your whole life waiting for something to happen, sometimes you have to make it happen.

Red to black

May the balance sheet of your life always be in the black.

Back to basics

Can't lament the past, have to learn from it and move on.

Chase of life

Chasing time = chasing money = chasing life.

Stop the merry-go-round.

Children of the light

That is what we are.

Coming home

About time. Don't you think?

Revisions of life

My life is a poem, I'm constantly revising….

Journey of a lifetime

From where we've come to where we are…

Measure your words, thoughts and actions with the greatest of care – they're eternal – just like you.

No charge

Service isn't something you can put a price tag on….

Needs of life

I have more than enough of everything I will ever need ~ light is all I need….

It's time

K nock, knock, Akal Sahai, it's time to find some income….

Best mates

T hey stand by you through thick and thin. When all appears lost they stick with you and remind you, "Nothing is lost, it'll be okay."

Nothing is lost, it'll be okay, I promise.

New friends

" *H* ope your inspiration lasts for ages," sweetest thing anyone has said to me in a long time….

Found a nickel made in 1940 – 7 decades ago… I wonder, of what lands it's seen and the people it's met on its journey to my hand….

If it could, what would it tell me?

"Sat Nam."

Soap of life

*I*t doesn't matter what you would do differently if given the opportunity to do it all over again ~ it's all just soap down the drain.

∞

*L*et the energy grow and let's see what happens….

Formula of life

*T*hought + energy applied = creation.

Waters of life

See yourself as you would be, and fly through life!

Words of life

Dear friend who talks about sitting under my light, what a deep and profound honor, to know I've reached someone....

I would define my existence by these 4 words: I am the lighthouse.

You?

Definition of life

It's how we define ourselves that shapes our existence....

Philosopher's stone

My father recently referred to me as a philosopher... I never really thought of myself as a philosopher....

How do you think of yourself?

No fear here

You face your fears and you walk in the light, simple as that.

Sat Nam.

Hands of time

May they be kind to you.

Book of light

Life is an empty page and you are the pen, write what you would like and let the universe sort it out.

Sat Nam.

~

*G*reat deal of time writing of the light, my greatest desire ~ but whatever you think is best universe.

What's your greatest desire?

Way of the light

*T*o write of home and help others find their way, to bring a smile to someone's face, to hold them when they cry, to uplift everyone we meet, to move ever higher and feed their hunger for the light, to remind them they already know the way home – that's the way of the light.

Treasures of life

*F*riends are the most precious of commodities, treasure them ~ always.

Wellspring of life

When it flows we flourish, when it runs dry life runs dry....

Cup of light

May yours always be full.

One breathe, one life

Energy seems to rise of its own accord....

In the lobby

The light's always there, just waiting for you to find it.

Dancing partners

*M*eet me in the light.

Let go

*W*hat more can I say?

By the light

*L*ook for me there, and find yourself.

Look within

*W*e never find anything because we're always looking in the
wrong place. All the answers are within ~ unlock them.

Tilde of life

Life is like a ~ it's filled with waves, may you ride them well.

Order of the Light

Won't you join me?

I vow

To spend more time working on the goal and less time playing with distractions, this I vow.

Swayed by the light

I think consciousness and therefore enlightenment is measured by how much sway over you the distractions have....

Love's light

I want you to know something right now – I love you and a lot of other people do too.

Feathers of life

H ad the floating dream again the other night, think I'll just float away….

May you always float through life.

Let them out

L ight/all your highest dreams are already within you, you just have to let them out.

Get me out

H ome is where your sheepskin is, home is wherever you wrap your turban, everything in this life is all in your head – get out of it.

For Jacob

Physical ancestor – born 300 years before I – journeyed to this land at the age of 16… wonder what it was like….

Exercise in consciousness

Does this (what I am doing right now) raise my consciousness?

If not, then why am I doing it?

Body of light

Ego says, "How can I distract him now? In what way can I keep him from dealing with reality?"

That's what it does, the choice to serve others is kryptonite to the ego, it's what breaks the ego's power over you.

Fly straight!

Bless them

*I*f during the interview they explain, "You have to leave your soul at the door," well, I'm here to uplift you.

Compassion is the root of my soul, we travel together.

Sat Nam.

Let it out

*T*rilogy of light draws to a close, fantasy novel wants out, light shines through in service to all….

Warriors of light, monsters, swords, magic and all that, just waiting to be written, just like life, you just have to let it out.

On the ledge

*D*ove, seated atop her 3rd pair of eggs – on a chair on my balcony no less, on a ledge of the lighthouse….

Priorities of light

More time working for the light and less time playing with distractions, listening to the voice of the soul rather than the ego, elevating everyone rather than stumbling around in the dark myself, those are my priorities of light.

Sat Nam.

Automatic

At every choice, every action, every thought, "Does this serve the light, or is this the ego?" VERY soon, won't even be a question, it'll be automatic.

Conscious

Breathe consciously and you will always be ~ conscious.

Whatever it takes

*L*eft the maya and ego behind and dove into the light within.

Service, before myself.

Whatever it takes….

Help

*I*deas are flowing, how about some income?

"Write it."

Come back

*F*arther from reality you move, farther away from your dreams you are.

Gateway to Infinity

Step through it, I'll see you on the other side.

Truth of life

Escape our karma we cannot, can only hope to burn it off.

May yours be paid in full.

Facts of life

Only one person's gonna move you through this life and that's you.

Well of light

May we all find it....

One race

*T*he human race.

Destinations of light

*Y*ou're only as far away as you think you are.

Revisions of light

*V*eil between what is real and what is not lifts… seeing things that were always and yet never there, that's what life is about, finding our way back to the light within.

May we all live happily ever after.

Sat Nam.

The Truth

Destined to walk among the stars, that is what we are.

Magic

Fear of never gaining that which I did not have, that which I so wanted kept me away from it all, until a boy named Harry led me into the light.

They who live without fear walk in the eternal light.

All of it

Growth ~ it's not about what meditation you do or how much yoga you do, it's about how much you're willing to let go of….

A New Hope

Here's to hope, may it reign supreme.

Bless you Sister, thank you

Sister blessed me, "Good luck to you," she said as we parted company….

Good luck to you all, may your days be many and may your journey into the Light be a blessed one.

Sat Nam.

Four years on

No finer thing upon this land, than the adventures of Mister Harry James Potter and his friends, Miss Hermione Granger and Mister Ronald Weasley ☺ Nothing more can I say, no higher Truth can I speak, than this:

May their courage be yours –

May your friendships be as True and strong as theirs –

May you always place others before yourself –

May you always walk in the light –

And may we meet, on our journey home, our journey into the Light.

~Sat Nam,

Akal Sahai Singh (Steve Coffing)

It has been my deepest honor, sharing my journey with you. May the long time sun ever shine upon you.

~Sat Nam.

Epilogue

Almost 4 years to the day since I started writing *Be the Lighthouse*…9/9/09… such symmetry….

Life itself is change, grow with it.

Inspiration is where it finds you.

Embrace the perfection in all things.

Breathe, forgive, release all anger and change your destiny you will.

Until next time ~ Sat Nam.

Decisions… decisions

The world that I as Mr. S. Coffing was born into is vastly different from the one that I as Akal Sahai Singh with the super fierce beard live, breathe, write this and say, 'Sat Nam,' in.

Now I am obviously not 2 people but obviously walk in both worlds.

In one, my beard receives glowing praise all around, in the other… it varies.

Children often make this face like they think I'm Santa Claus, adults, well, the praise as I am oft reminded, doesn't come from the hiring manager….

Well, I'm in the wrong world then and yes, I am keeping the super fierce beard!

The most

Ultimately, I think, that all we can do is be the best person we possibly can each and every moment we are blessed to draw breath.

May you always make the most of yours.

~Sat Nam.

October 21, 2009

Bound Lotus, Day 1500…

Fascinating number….

Wanted the trilogy of light to end on a high note – enlightenment, true and lasting love, financial prosperity… the good is always there though and yes you have to play the hand you're dealt.

What I can say is, everything I don't need for the journey home – fear, doubt, want, need, lack, judgment, negativity – I dropped it all in the River of Truth and I'm sailing home now.

You're perfect just the way you are and I love you just the way you are.

~Sat Nam.

For Jackson

We all have our own journey to make, may yours lead you unto to light.

~Sat Nam

Deed to the Light

It's not about whatever it is I think I need, it's about whatever gets me home.

Whatever you think is best Infinite.

~Sat Nam.

Novel of life

I like happy endings ~ write yours.

Love is

What is love?

Love is why you get up in the morning, love is why you breathe, love is why you live, love is why the light shines.

~Sat Nam

12/16/09

Remember to breathe and leave everything to the universe.

For Lee

Friend commented on how he could fit everything he truly needed into a duffle bag… got me to wondering….

Notebook, pen, water bottle, Swiss Army knife, yoga mat, sheepskin, change of clothes, toothbrush, toothpaste, cell phone, charger….

Fascinating proposition, what we truly need versus what we have… lot of open space in my house….

Good times

You know those days where you just wanna just jump up and down and shout,
"WOOOOOOOOOOOOOOOOOOOOOOOOOOOOOOOOO
OOOOOOOO!!1!" I'm having that day right now ☺

Patience

I've waited 8 centuries, what's a few more days, what's a few more weeks?

Higher perspective

Neighbor was carried off in an ambulance… thought I had problems… thank you universe for giving me some perspective….

Hope she's okay….

May you

Ultimately, I think that's all any of us want, is something and someone to call our own... I'm here to tell you though, everything already is yours and the sad thing is, how few people will ever know, will ever touch that....

May you live it, may all your dreams and more be yours.

Sat Nam

Promises of Light

Sometimes you just need to know everything is going to be okay.

It will, I promise.

Ever higher

Neighbor still hasn't returned home....

Friend spoke of not having money to buy food for three days....

Read about a man who looked for quarters in the street so he could do laundry....

Thank you universe, for giving me some perspective....

May your perspective be, ever higher.

Patience pays

*H*ow long would you wait?

Until the end of time.

Then why are you worried?

Good question, Sat Nam.

Sat Nam.

2010

*T*he year of liberation, from anything and everything that no longer serves me. No more attachments to results, what will be will be....

Yes

I know in my heart that everything is going to be okay.

Yes it will, I guarantee it.

Sat Nam.

Sat Nam.

Signs of Light

*N*ow I am normally not one to believe in signs, portents or omens, but it is the middle of January and there is a pregnant dove on my balcony!

I know she's one of the doves from last year, returned to create new life… a good sign if ever there was one!

Dreams of flight

*H*ad the floating dream again last night, was real though….

I was awake, even felt the wind in my face as I floated above/through it all… as if the Infinite were saying, "*I got this, I got your back.*"

May you float through life.

~Sat Nam.

Home sweet home

"*O*h, oh, now you pick us up!*" My notebook and pen start in on me as we sit down to write.

"*You leave us sitting in the closet –*"

It's better than the floor.

"There is that," they say in agreement.

So what would you 2 like to tell the world this night?

"It just is. What will be will be."

Goodnight.

"Goodnight."

Have faith

God told me the world would be mine if I would but have faith.

~Sat Nam.

Living it

Bound Lotus, Day 1600….

Don't think there's anything else I could ever say, just that Bound Lotus is the best/truest friend/teacher I've ever had: patience, surrender, faith, strength and keeping up are what life is all about.

~Sat Nam.

I am what I am

I think that's the greatest lesson in life – enjoying what is there rather than wanting what is not.

~Sat Nam.

In class

T hank you Wyatt and Ruud, for bringing some laughter into my life at a much needed moment.

Next week we'll do a thousand frogs!

For the future

W as attached to an ideal, to an outcome that I wanted, that I've always wanted, but then again, it was never mine to begin with… God promised it will be, no timeline on that though… patient you must be, for the yogi it is time to wait as well.

More to let go of there is….

That man

Long time ago in a land far, far away there was a man who lived in a lighthouse.

God told the man, *"Keep the light and the world will be yours."*

So every night the light shined bright as the man tended to the lighthouse.

Eventually he grew old and one day, no longer able to climb the stairs, he left his body, one with the universe. I would like to be that man.

Truisms of Light

Want, attachment, I don't care anymore, what will be will be, and what I will be is the lighthouse!

Definitions of Light

Always wanted what I didn't have… no point in holding on to what was never there!

Untitled

"Thank you for the friend I made, please watch over her as you've watched over me," no higher Truth may I speak, in no higher way can I honor her friendship. ~Sat Nam.

Be happy!

Now it's time to dance and sing Wahe Guru, something my pen has always wanted to do!

Reality

Let it come to you, chase it and you end up chasing your own tail.

When doves fly

The doves love my balcony, sometimes I think they come just to remind me it will all be okay, that it's not about what I want or don't have, that it's about being thankful and grateful for what I do have and leaving it all to the Infinite. Those are some wise doves!

One

*B*ound stretches the mind, it's that whole impossible task thing, it is impossible, it's literally not possible, until it is, just one more inch, just one more minute, just one more breath, just one more tear, just one more thing to let go of, just one more fear to drop, that's all life is, just one moment at a time....

Flexibility

*T*he mind needs stretching, not the body.

For Balprem

*T*hat's what Bound is, you're dying, it's the hardest thing there is to do, the mind/body/ego rails, **GET ME OUT** or whatever, yet you do it anyway, that's what being the lighthouse is all about, you're not doing it for yourself, you're doing it for them and when you realize, "Them," is the entire world, you've already arrived at your destination.

~Sat Nam

Keeping up

*T*he first day was the easy day. It's dying and doing it again the next day, that's the hard part, but you do it anyway, that's what it's all about!

I do what I can

A friend wrote, "Peering at the Lighthouse," fully aware of the title of my first book…. I don't really think of myself as anything in particular, like Bob Leckie said, I do what I can ☺

In my hands

*T*here it was, in one golden moment, I realized I already had everything I'd ever wanted, had been too busy chasing my own tail to realize it was right there in my hands all along….

May all your moments be golden.

~Sat Nam.

Found

To Jack and Kate, may you forever live in the moment of Love.

~Sat Nam.

Psst

The thing you've forgotten is that you are the magic.

To do list

Spent more than half my life chasing something I didn't really need… I've got more important things to do….

Hello old friend

Don't deny your humanity, embrace your divinity!

~Be the Lighthouse~

Something I'd wanted for decades was set before me, to my complete disinterest, got more important things to do….
~~~~~~Be the Lighthouse~~~~~~

WWID

What would Iva do?

Hold herself to the purity of the Light.

~~~~~~

Questions of Light

What's more important, pleasures of the flesh, or serving all life?

~~~~~~
~~~~~~

Or what?

What is the meaning of Life?

Why did you come to this plane, this Earth?

To serve all life, to make this world a better place, to be there in the night for someone to reach out to, to bring a smile to the face of someone in pain?

Or?

What did I do?

If you were to ask yourself, "Did I uplift enough?"

What would your answer be, and how happy with that answer would you be?

Take it with you

Making a difference in the life of another, now that's something you can truly take with you into the next life!

To the brim

*I*f a thing uplifts the spirit, then it truly is a good thing.

May your life be filled to the brim with good things.

Prison of Light

*T*he prison is in your mind, the limitations those we place upon ourselves.

Have it

*H*ealing is about faith, have it ~~~~

In the Light

*S*ome will refuse your help, no matter how sorely they are in need/or how freely it is offered.

Shine on ~~~~

For Mallory

Words I wrote 6 plus years past, ring truer now than ever:

"–as Mallory had said, letting go was the key to it all, for in the release of all attachments came complete freedom."

So the question has to be, what are you attached to?

Your humble servant,

–Akal Sahai

Dreams of Light

Whatever you do in this life, follow your dreams.

~Back~

Once upon a time, the angel's playground was a physical place I visited. Then it became a state of mind… one that I seemed to have lost along the way.

Thank you Harpartap and Hari Bhajan for helping me to find my way back.

Lighten up

We need to laugh more.

Hit the mat

Yet to discover a problem yoga couldn't solve… not that it resolves the relevant conundrum, rather that is dissolves my thoughts about it.

Time to hit the mat!

Letters to Infinity I

Dear Infinite Universe,

Hello, how are you doing today?

Happy and yet sad.

Me too… I would like to rise above the trials and tribulations of this life, I would like to bless all, particularly those who wish me harm.

You just did. The lighthouse has no enemies, only those who oppose the Light, the Truth. You live in a world where it is easier to blame everything on someone else.

I know, I also know I chose this life.

That you did, creating your own experience you are. It's not what someone else does that matters, it's your experience of it that does. They cannot hurt you, only you can. Violence/words/whatever, do not matter, bless them all and be the lighthouse. Sat Nam.

Sat Nam.

Stand Tall

Being the lighthouse isn't about everybody loving you, it's about standing tall whether they love you or they throw rocks at you.

May we all have more of the former and less of the later.

Indifference of Light

Lighthouse doesn't react, it just shines.

Be the lighthouse.

Be, more

People throw rocks at the lighthouse because it doesn't react, because it's something they're not – more.

What are you?

It doesn't really matter whether you are loved, appreciated or hated, it's how you feel about who and what you are that matters, not what anyone else thinks.

Games of Life

The name of the game is anger and life feeds it: the squeeze, the pressure, the play, the push, the hurrying and scurrying frantic pace of "modern" life.

The name of the game is peace and the light feeds it.

What game you play is up to you.

Play well ☺

Tell me

How many times would you die to save the Universe?

How many times would you die to save someone who could not defend themselves?

How hard would you try to cross the street?

Does your soul cry out in the night, wanting to be and do more, to be liberated from ___________ ?

Ultimate Triumph

Let the war be with yourself and not them, hold the arms up and triumph for all time!

Arms up!

Their struggles are not yours.

#2

Neutrality before all else.

For Zus

There's always room for one more.

Thanksgiving

Thank you for the beauty that I have known and seen. Thank you for the angelic music of Singh Kaur, thank you for all of my loving friends and family, thank you for my good health and prosperity, thank you for the love I have known and every pain I have ever felt so that I may appreciate my Infinite blessings all the more.

Most of all, thank you for helping me to be the lighthouse so that I may serve all.

Sat Nam,

Akal Sahai Singh

November 20, 2010

Wish list

Dear Universe,

I would like to be the most neutral, calmest, laid back, easy going being in the history of the Universe.

Bless you, thank you.

~Sat Nam.

The Zone

Very little exists in the zone, yet it's the place where I dwell.

What I do not have, matters not, what is important is that I am, I am, and what I am most of all is deeply and profoundly grateful for all that I am and all that I will ever be, have, see or do.

~Sat Nam.

?

I began to wonder, if angels felt our pain, and I was instantly saddened, yet I had nothing to be sad about....

Love is all around us, so the question is, why would one not feel it?

For Guru Sandesh

Originally, the question was, "What troubles an angel on this cool Solstice eve?" <but> What I realized, was that she visited to teach me, that the question actually is, "How can I serve you?" And that if we all live by that question, no one will ever have troubles again.

There are not words upon this plane to express my gratitude for what you have shown me Guru Sandesh, I realize now, that, where I seek to be, I've been there all along, I just didn't realize it.

~Sat Nam.

For Daljit

"You look like a Guru my friend. You could be the next Osho."

Far and away, the most amazingly beautiful words ever spoken to me, I still bask in their glow.

Infinite blessings upon you and your family Daljit Singh Ji!

For Siri Amar Dev

Words that move me in the night, words that move me into the Light, words that move me through life....

How to express all that is, in a few short words, how to express the Infinite gratitude that accompanies the awakening call of one's destiny, how to express the certainty, that one's next step is the correct one? You trust in the light and you do it.

Thank you Siri Amar Dev, for ever being my friend.

Days gone by

*B*ound Lotus, Day 1933

With great laughter, I read of my pen and its fondness for my notebook, of a specific time when I thought a great thing would happen, and actually it did, just not in the way I expected.

I wrote of prosperity I'd not yet received and that which I was meditating for, all part of the journey to understanding, that, it was actually the Bound Lotus and the work it does on the radiant body that was bringing all of these wonderful opportunities to me.

Maybe I'd thought, great rivers of cash would rain down upon me and maybe they will at some point, but, you have to work for prosperity!

I bow to thee

*I*t's the student who is actually the teacher.

Life/Bound Lotus

*I*t's about stretching the mind until anything is possible.

In the Stillness

*I*t's all about penetrating the mind.

What to do....

*A*gain the conundrum became, what to share with the world... if it spoke my Truth yes, but – *Why is there a but?*

Because, they're love poems written about a relationship that ended.

All relationships end, everything upon this plane is transitory.

I specifically mention her name, several times.

You wrote about a woman who broke your heart and yet you published those writings.

Without her name.

What's the problem?

I wrote of things that made me laugh, things that warmed my heart and touched my soul....

Miracles of Light

That 3rd miracle arrived some two years later in the form of the job of my dreams and the fascinating thing was that it wasn't about the relationship that had ended, it was about the myriad relationships that I **<did>** have – be they friends, family, co-workers or otherwise and how I could best serve them.

Looking Forward

Fascinating, reading back, of how I'd written of exactly how and what I wished my life to be then, seeing now, how it had all unfolded….

Reminders of Light

It will benefit no one if you share not the pain....

Life isn't about the good times, it's the trying times and how we handle them that define our existence.

If I could serve one person by sharing something that happened to me, it will have been worth it.

It's not about where I am, it's where I was at that moment.

Ultimately, I would like to think, I wrote of hope and the desire to be and do more, to better serve – everyone.

May we all walk in the light together.

~Sat Nam.

Until Next Time

To sum it all up, this is my journey, thank you for being a part of it!

Resources

For more information on Bound Lotus, please visit Mahan Kirn Kaur Khalsa's website at www.boundlotus.com

To find a KRI Certified Instructor near you, please visit the International Kundalini Yoga Teachers Association (IKYTA) website at www.kundaliniyoga.com.

For more information on Kundalini Yoga Events visit www.3ho.org

For Kundalini Yoga products and Yogi Bhajan DVDs visit www.a-healing.com

CPSIA information can be obtained at www.ICGtesting.com
231564LV00001B/129/P